Best Wishes

Pam Mayan

IN THE COMPANY OF FLOWERS

Ron Morgan

Photographs by Keith Lewis

Half Full Press

Oakland, California

IN THE COMPANY OF FLOWERS

For information, please contact:
Half Full Press
1814 Franklin Street, Suite 820
Oakland, CA 94612
(510) 839-5471

Book Designer/Editor: Annabelle Louie
Assistant Editor: Joan Lee

Printed and Bound in China

ISBN 0-9719552-3-9

FIRST EDITION

Dedicated to the Garden Club

ladies of the world,

without whose encouragement and enthusiasm

this book would have never been possible.

The work that you do collectively

makes our small world immensely more

beautiful, inviting and inspiring.

I am deeply and forever in your debt.

CONTENTS

FOREWORD

As a faithful attendee of garden club lectures, aspiring floral designer and devoted fan of Ron Morgan, I have never encountered anyone who can begin to match Ron's wit, creativity and impeccable sense of color and design. On dozens of occasions, I have watched him astound audiences as he dashes off one remarkable table setting after another, all the while mesmerizing attendees with a self-effacing patter of humor and insights into design. He accomplishes this as he keeps his eyes on a rapt audience, with little apparent attention being given to the flowers he is arranging. Then, without fanfare, Ron suddenly wheels the completed creation towards the audience. His masterpieces are invariably greeted by a universal burst of applause, astonishment and unbridled glee.

Where or how Ron comes up with his unique ideas is anyone's guess, but I know full well that they are essentially spontaneous. For a far-off lecture, he simply tells his hosts to bring a dozen or so containers of their choice. Neither party specifies size, color, theme or any of the specifics regarding the lecture. Upon arrival, he visits local flower and produce markets, and, while en route to the lecture, he will stop along the road—possibly the manicured front lawn belonging to someone who will be in the audience—and pick something that will add a truly local touch. Apart from a stage full of flowers and containers, the beginning canvas is blank—there are no notes or sketches that act as a guide or template. Minutes later, there are magnificent table settings that no one, including Ron, has ever envisioned before.

Having known Ron for 30 years, the artistic attribute that impresses me most is his incredible grasp of color. The remarkable and ever-subtle blend of colors in this book are a perfect testament to that uncanny ability. Somewhere in the far recesses of his fertile mind, he is able to envision how various elements of a table setting will interact before he even starts the actual selection of the various elements. Working with this mental picture, he can magically combine five different types of flowers, two or three fruits or vegetables, a container, various selections of greenery, plates, glasses and other table accessories into tablescape with a coherent theme where everything is in exquisite harmony.

Ron is an artist whose mastery of colors, creativity and enthusiasm inspire us mortals to believe that we too can create works that reflect our own innate talents and insights. This is essentially the underlying theme of Ron's lectures as well—don't get hung up on the details, be yourself, have fun and go for it!

Leslie Bond

ART
IN THE
GARDEN

Berry Sweet

Say Hello to Summer

Use Good Scents

Uninvited Guests

Simple Abundance

Captive Audience

CULTURAL

CREATIONS

Fish Tales

The Look of Lushness

Rain or Shine

Not All
Art
Comes
in a
Frame

Above and Beyond

Rhapsody in Red

SPIRITUAL

RETREAT

Sweet

Serenity

Tall, Dark and Handsome

A Fine Catch

Water Power

Crystal Clear

Multiple Complements

FLIGHTS

OF

FANCY

Out in the Open

Avant Garden

Strange Bedfellows

Handle Gingerly

It's A Small World

POTPOURRI

Aromatherapy

A Tisket, A Tasket,

A Green and Yellow Basket

Cherry-ish the Memories

A
Warm
and
Sunny
Disposition

A Slice of Life

Room With a View

CORNUCOPIA

Green with Envy

Holiday Harvest

Citrus Heights

Bring Home the Beach

Party in a Pear Tree

Birds
of
a
Feather

IN
FOR THE
EVENING

Around and Around We Go!

Process of Illumination

Rooted

Branching Out

Snow Drift

Two's Company

Ties That Bind

Ripple Effect

MAGICAL
MOTIFS

Jungle

Story

Pheasantly Surprised

Dinner
With
Old
Friends

Midas Touch

In the Arms of Angels

Glass Menagerie

Great Oaks From Little Acorns Grow

DOUBLE
TAKES

Sushi Garden

Please Pass the Pepper

Polka Dot Parade

Veggie Patch

All Choked Up!

A Walk

in the Park

Ruler of

the Roost

IN THE COMPANY OF FLOWERS

Flowers have always been the focal point of my life. Fortunately, as I explored this passion, I have never lacked for exceptional company. Garden clubs around the country are full of people who share my zeal for flowers, gardens and arrangements. I have not only made lifelong friendships with many such members, but I have been privileged to share my ideas, arrangements and methods with the clubs around the country that have invited me to give lectures.

My lecturing career began when the goddess of fortune handed me an irresistible challenge. It all began about 40 years ago, when the National Garden Club Convention took place in my stomping grounds of Oakland, California. My garden club ladies brought me to see a Mrs. Schulke of Cleveland, Ohio, give a talk and demonstration. Mrs. Schulke was the Grand Dame of flower arrangements, and she impressed upon her audience the importance of following very rigid rules in making centerpieces. The arrangement's height could only be 1.5 times the width, everything had to be perfectly proportional, no artificial accessories could be used and so on.

Well, rules and formalities have never been my strong suit, and, by an odd twist of fate, I got the chance to show everyone what I would do instead. On the following night of the convention, a friend and I made plans to see another demonstration. The scheduled lecturer, however, broke her arm, and my friend volunteered me in her stead. What followed was a sleepless and anxious night of preparation, far too many broken rules and, ultimately, a delighted audience. Going against convention, I made an arrangement that was extremely tall and thin. I used figurines that were also a no-no, but I showed the audience how much fun coloring outside of the lines could be. While the arrangement didn't conform to traditional standards, it was a hit nonetheless.

As it so happens, the resident authority, Mrs. Schulke, was in the audience. To my relief, she was not offended that I had haphazardly broken all of her rules. On the contrary, she was so impressed that she invited me to be a lecturer for her garden club in Cleveland, Ohio. I delivered my first lecture at the Halle Brothers Department Store. After that, word of mouth led to my giving hundreds of lectures around the Garden Club lecture circuit, both nationally and internationally.

Traveling around the country to visit garden clubs has allowed me to see the most incredible gardens and houses, as well as become great friends with their owners. I thrive on meeting new people at lectures all the time, because everyone who belongs to a garden club is, by definition, lovely. I truly believe that people who nourish plants are nice people. Most people who garden are also interested in flower arranging, and so we've cultivated a common interest in collecting unique items for centerpieces by visiting antique shows and estate sales together. The end result is that the garden clubs and their members have brought me a lifelong exchange of ideas and lasting friendships.

Lectures have given me many wonderful, funny and unusual memories to cherish. At a lecture in Santa Barbara, California, they told me to just bring flowers and myself, and they would provide all the containers. The twist was that they were going to bring all their "problem containers" and ask me to figure out a way to use them. When I arrived, I realized I had an enormous problem on my hands. I had to break the news to them gently—just because something has a hole in it doesn't mean it was meant to hold flowers. Sometimes it's just there to be decorative. One of the ladies in the audience was holding a hideously shaped urn, and I hoped throughout the whole lecture that she wouldn't ask me what to do with it. However, she finally stood up and brought it forward. I told her that the thing was so ugly, all that could be done was just to drop it and break it. And so she did.

Lectures around the country have presented unique challenges that have, at times, boggled my mind. On occasion, time and material restrictions have forced me to consider using materials I never would have ordinarily considered and the end result is a far cry from what I had planned. When I was visiting Florida for a lecture, I didn't realize that the state had restrictions on bringing in plants—as in, they didn't allow any. After I arrived safely but my flowers had not, I went for a very long walk. I walked around the hotel parking lot and explored their lawns; I investigated the gardens surrounding the shopping center; and I finished up at the produce section of the supermarket. Somehow, with the help of pilfered flowers, wild foliage and the freshest fruits and vegetables around, it all worked out beautifully. At another lecture in Buffalo, New York, we were all trapped inside the hotel because it was freezing outside. This time, the flowers had arrived, but they were, unfortunately, frozen. I ended up raiding the hotel kitchen, not for survival goods, but for potatoes, cabbage, and any other edible goods that I could use in a centerpiece. And again, it worked. Even if nothing happens as you had originally planned, creativity and innovation can generally do the trick.

In fact, a time came when a little ingenuity went the extra distance. One of the biggest challenges I have had was auditioning to be a speaker at the Philadelphia Flower Show, the premiere floral event in the nation—if not the world. Not only was I late to my audition, but having just arrived from the airport, I had to leave my luggage on the side of the stage where I was setting up my arrangement. Unfortunately, as I worked on the arrangement, I noticed that the grapes had lost their luster. I wanted them to appear in their natural state, as if they were still lying on the stem in the sun, untouched by human hands. So I asked the judges to be patient, and I dashed off stage and pulled my shaving kit out of my luggage. Out came my odorless powder deodorant, which I sprinkled all over the grapes to give them that gray, natural sheen that I wanted. After the judges stopped laughing, they were suitably impressed and they gave me the job.

For years I had been talking about getting a book done, but it wasn't until 2002 that THE CENTER OF ATTENTION, my first book, was finally completed and published. I was grateful because the attendees of my lectures were the first to sign up and ask for a copy. In fact, the total number of lectures mushroomed, and I felt like a garden club rock star, signing books and visiting many, many more clubs and people than ever before. I also began getting calls from museums, junior leagues and hospitals asking me to lecture, proving that anyone from anywhere can appreciate the art of flower arranging. I often lecture at new clubs where I have never been before, but I still return to garden clubs that I've previously visited. Flower arranging never gets old and neither do the friendships that I've made.

It was only natural then that I try my hand at another book, and IN THE COMPANY OF FLOWERS is the fruit (and flower) of those labors. I couldn't resist the opportunity to immortalize even more outrageous centerpieces. This time around, I wanted to be a bit more playful and creative, whether it was by adding animal figurines or flourishes of ginger and asparagus. Whereas creating THE CENTER OF ATTENTION gave me a rather nerve-wracking introduction to the world of publishing, IN THE COMPANY OF FLOWERS was more of a relaxing interlude during which I could concentrate on ways to turn the art of creating centerpieces upside down.

For all the fun offered by the world of flower arranging, floral centerpieces have a remarkably practical use when entertaining guests. When clients ask for help decorating their house for a party, I always think of the centerpiece first, because that's also what the guests first notice. This is an opportunity to exercise your creative side, yet you can easily keep it casual. When I'm having a party, working with the centerpiece is always the most exciting part, so I save it for last. I often end up being inspired by the food that I'm preparing, which makes its way into the centerpiece in various forms. This is how I end up making centerpieces like sushi rolls made from flowers and not fish, bell peppers that become tulips and carnations that are transformed into cauliflowers. Of course, these centerpieces are paired with main dishes like sushi rolls that are actually edible, bell pepper salsas and cauliflower salad. Guests will look down at the food on their plate, then at the food used in the centerpiece and back again. It's wonderful fun when the eye can connect two or three things together. In that manner, flower arranging is a lot like fashion and decorating rooms. It's all about the coordination of color among whatever items are being used—the napkins, food, china, centerpiece and so on.

When shopping for materials to use in a centerpiece, I look at everything with different eyes. Browsing in a grocery store, I'm not concerned about an item's taste or nutritional value, but rather shape and color. The spectrum of colors available continues to inspire me and brings me back to creating arrangements again and again. I prefer to focus on the use of one dominant color, and there are no limits in sight for the kinds of blends that can be made. I avoid mixing colors because that confuses the eye, and after all, the arrangement is not a patchwork quilt. Even when focusing on one color, flowers offer an endless amount of possibilities.

I like to keep flower arranging fun, creative and simple, because there's nothing that gets tiring about that. Don't ever get too serious or caught up in too many rules; remind yourself to have a good time and just open your mind. Walk around in the morning and look not just for flowers, but foliage, berries and other plants. Flowers are easy to obtain, but they always need the right kind of foliage to surround and complement them. Walk through yards, pretend to tie your shoe and examine someone's bushes. The best pieces are often slightly ill-gotten. My most valuable purchase ever has been a $4 orange freeway worker's vest. Wearing it, I can stop anywhere on the freeway and pick out whatever I like.

I hope everyone walks away from seeing one of my lectures or going through this book thinking, "I can do that." It's incredibly uplifting to have someone walk into your home and express admiration for a stunning centerpiece. You can say, oh-so-modestly, "I did that." I hope everyone experiences this exhilarating feeling and sense of accomplishment.

COMMENTARY

ON

THE

DESIGNS

	Front Cover	IN THE COMPANY OF FLOWERS CONTAINER: Antique Indian offering tray. MATERIAL: Roses, lilies, zinnias, castor bean pods, hypericum, berries and anemonies.	The lushness and full bloom of the strong summer flowers create a rich and exuberant arrangement.
	Title Page	ART OF REFLECTION CONTAINER: Glass soufflé dishes. MATERIAL: Ficus leaves, plums, hypericum berries, dahlias, gerber daisies and castor bean seeds.	The sunny patio and all the red seat coverings demanded the red color scheme. The Mediterranean feeling of the terrace did the rest.
	12 - 13	BERRY SWEET CONTAINER: Terra cotta urn and terra cotta pots. MATERIAL: Strawberries, hypericum leaves and blackberries.	The fragile strawberries against the rough terra cotta pots provide a great textural foil. The contrast of smooth against rough creates all the fun.
	14 - 15	SAY HELLO TO SUMMER CONTAINER: Glass compote. MATERIAL: Tulips, jack-in-the-pulpit pods, dahlias, roses, viburnum and celocia.	The abundance and bright colors of summer flowers are best bunched and made to look lush and beautiful.
	16 - 19	USE GOOD SCENTS CONTAINER: Large amethyst dish and old terra cotta capital. MATERIAL: Roses, hydrangea, purple beans, oregano, sweet peas and purple artichokes.	An outdoor summer luncheon and the overpowering fragrances were the key! The combination of the sweetness of the flowers against the pungent aroma of the oregano will enhance the flavor of the lunch.
	20 - 23	UNINVITED GUESTS CONTAINER: Wicker basket. MATERIAL: Hydrangea, kale, persimmons, green tomatoes and kiwi fruit.	The lime green of the old frog figurine collection provided the inspiration to gather all the green materials and bunch them in the basket for an outdoor setting.

24 - 25 SIMPLE ABUNDANCE
CONTAINER: Asparagus tied to tin pail.
MATERIAL: Asparagus, roses, ranunculus, pink japonica buds and poppy pods.

The tight bundling of the asparagus calls for a very controlled use of flowers, giving the feeling of a bunch of flowers tied together by their stems.

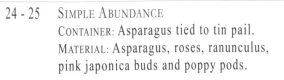

26 - 27 CAPTIVE AUDIENCE
CONTAINER: Two sizes of glass cylinders.
MATERIAL: Tulips and pillar candles.

Place one cylinder inside the other and then insert pillar candles into the smaller cylinder. Adding a ring of tulips growing inside the second cylinder creates a simple and elegant look.

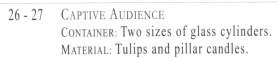

30 - 33 FISH TALES
CONTAINER: Large glass cylinder.
MATERIAL: Rocks, seashells, coral, succulents and ficus leaves.

The color and texture of the antique wallpaper screen and wonderful majolica collection inspired this underwater garden.

34 - 37 THE LOOK OF LUSHNESS
CONTAINER: Old blue and white sake cups.
MATERIAL: Hydrangea, delphinium, hyacinths and tweedia.

Blue on blue on blue. Stick to a single color and repeat it again and again and again. All materials stuck in a vertical position create the visual effect of bringing the outdoors inside.

38 - 41 RAIN OR SHINE
CONTAINER: Wooden base from temple figure.
MATERIAL: Castor beans, dahlias, orchids, hypericum, croton leaves and tei leaves.

Placing an umbrella in the middle of the table with top lighting gave a wonderful, intimate effect to a large table. The wall carving in the background was paramount to the coloring of the flowers and accessories.

42 - 45 NOT ALL ART COMES IN A FRAME
CONTAINER: Pin holders and antique art deco figurine.
MATERIAL: Calla lilies and sun flower heads.

The classic, simple lines of the figurine require restraint and simplicity in the flowers. The one sunflower head wired to her hand adds to the whimsy.

46 - 47 ABOVE AND BEYOND
CONTAINER: Black wooden pepper grinders with tops removed.
MATERIAL: Gilded bamboo, orchids and croton leaves.

Simple, simple. Containers filled with gilded bamboo branches and a few orchids tucked in at the base are finished off with leaves. The gilded bamboo repeats the china pattern.

48 - 51 RHAPSODY IN RED
CONTAINER: Two Japanese red lacquer lantern bases.
MATERIAL: Red coral, rose hips, hypericum berries, blackberries and crab apples.

Red was the obvious way to go in this room. The use of all shades of lacquer reds, small berries tucked into cone shapes, and topped with Italian drapery rod finials, give a festive flair.

54 - 57 SWEET SERENITY
CONTAINER: Chinese scrolls, antique buddhas and pin holders.
MATERIAL: Dried lotus leaves, tree of heaven, cymbidium orchids, ficus leaves and aralia leaves.

One of the buddhas is placed higher than the other to create a dramatic effect. Both appear to be surrounded by the lush jungle growth of the plant materials.

58 - 59 TALL, DARK AND HANDSOME
CONTAINER: Japanese stands and shallow black saucers.
MATERIAL: Equisetum and calla lilies.

The simple sophistication of bundled sections of reeds and calla lilies peeking out creates a clean and dramatic effect.

60 - 63 A FINE CATCH
CONTAINER: Antique Chinese ceramic fish.
MATERIAL: Bittersweet zinnias, scabiosa pods and black-eyed susan pods.

The fish seems to be swimming through a bed of seaweed in search of dinner. The deeper pods repeat the black eye of the fish, completing the coordination of materials and container.

64 - 65 WATER POWER
CONTAINER: Glass rectangles.
MATERIAL: Acorns, succulents, dahlias and lotus pods.

Submerging materials in the water and having the reflective effect of leaves and flowers placed on both sides of the container adds to the third dimension. The lily pods seem to be growing naturally out of the pond.

| 66 - 67 | CRYSTAL CLEAR
CONTAINER: Flat and cubed glass containers.
MATERIAL: Plastic snow flakes and white naked ladies. | The wintry effect of the snow flakes submerged in water and a sparse amount of plant material create a cool winter effect, simply and elegantly. |

| 68 - 69 | MULTIPLE COMPLEMENTS
CONTAINER: Chinese ginger jars.
MATERIAL: Poppy pods, ranunculus and cabbage. | The grey green of the jars was the key to the color scheme. The cabbage and poppy pods are a perfect repeat of the color of the china and containers and the accent of the ranunculus is wonderful in color and shape to repeat the already round forms. |

| 72 - 73 | OUT IN THE OPEN
CONTAINER: Antique French iron planter.
MATERIAL: French cement mushrooms and lily of the valley. | The contrast of textures is what makes this so much fun. The rough cement of the mushrooms and the rough iron against one of nature's most delicate flowers are a wonderful exaggeration of textures. |

| 74 - 77 | AVANT GARDEN
CONTAINER: Woven birch.
MATERIAL: Birch, tulips, hyacinths, sweet peas and ranunculus. | Birch bark, cut into strips and glued onto the container, repeats the pattern of the woven china. The table is actually a living ivy topiary. All the flowers, organized in like kinds, and nestled among the ivy, add to the overall natural effect. |

| 78 - 79 | STRANGE BEDFELLOWS
CONTAINER: Antique terra cotta planter.
MATERIAL: Tomatoes, rose hips and tulips. | Color is everything – the red of the tomatoes exactly echoes the red of the open center of the tulips. The rose hips repeat the round shape, as well as the color. |

| 80 - 81 | HANDLE GINGERLY
CONTAINER: Rusted sewer grate strainer.
MATERIAL: Hyacinths and ginger root. | To create the natural growing effect, the ginger roots are placed at the base of the arrangement to look like bulbs or rhizomes. |

82 - 85   IT'S A SMALL WORLD
CONTAINER: Wooden Japanese planter.
MATERIAL: Birch, tulips, companulas, mushrooms and natural moss.

All materials seem to be growing outside in a garden. The scene creates a very natural miniature landscape.

88 - 91   AROMATHERAPY
CONTAINER: Collection of antique majolica pitchers.
MATERIAL: Roses, hydrangeas, sweet peas and lavender blackberries.

All the colors of the majolicas and the quilted table top are pulled together with groups of one kind of flower in each pot. What makes it such a visual treat is the use of masses of flowers in each pot.

92 - 95   A TISKET, A TASKET, A GREEN AND YELLOW BASKET
CONTAINER: Old wicker basket.
MATERIAL: Acorns, green apples, protea, green carnations and skeletonized magnolia leaves.

Gather the fruits and nuts of the season, place them in a basket and tuck in a few fresh flowers of just the right color. Be selective on choices and amounts.

96 - 97   CHERRY-ISH THE MEMORIES
CONTAINER: Small faux cement urns.
MATERIAL: Rhododendron leaves, cherries and small berries.

Something as simple as a cherry can have a classic look if handled in a classic manner. The formal use of leaves and cherries as collars on the urns is a great new look for an old favorite.

98 - 101   A WARM AND SUNNY DISPOSITION
CONTAINER: Faux moss terra cotta urn.
MATERIAL: Figs, dates, artichokes, sunflowers, oregano, miniature persimmons and lemons.

All the produce and all the memories of Tuscany, artfully draped in a container in the middle of the table, bring back vacations of the past.

102 - 103   A SLICE OF LIFE
CONTAINER: Antique bronze compote.
MATERIAL: Cantaloupe, begonias, hypericum, ginkgo seed pods and kumquats.

The lush look of the colors and the fragrance of the fresh melons make for a very inviting party.

215

104 - 107 ROOM WITH A VIEW
CONTAINER: Old bronze planter.
MATERIAL: Succulents, tweedia, anemonies and muscari.

The colors and textures melded perfectly with the patina of the bronze and the grey of the succulents. These colors are enhanced by the blues and purples to make an exciting combination.

110 - 113 GREEN WITH ENVY
CONTAINER: Faux cement urn.
MATERIAL: Limes, green persimmons, stephanotis on vine, tallow berries and society garlic.

The classical topiary shape and all the right chartreuse greens are a perfect complement to the red walls of the dining room. Candlesticks, also of fruit and flowers, help elongate the table. The stephanotis on vine, woven throughout the design, connects the various elements.

114 - 115 HOLIDAY HARVEST
CONTAINER: Old Japanese black lacquer square stand.
MATERIAL: Pomegranates, calla lilies, catoniaster, piris japonica, maple leaves and glass pears.

Fruits all harvested for the holiday. Some real, some not so real, add to the abundant feel of this tablescape for a warm holiday party.

116 - 119 CITRUS HEIGHTS
CONTAINER: Japanese bronze bowl.
MATERIAL: Oranges, cinnamon, rose hips, tangerines and miniature persimmons.

The old pomander and spices of the holidays get a fresh look, with oranges tied in ribbons, all mounded into topiary form, with cinnamon sticks and berries tucked in as finishing touches.

120 - 123 BRING HOME THE BEACH
CONTAINER: Antique wooden Italian gilded urn.
MATERIAL: Dates, zeringa berries, bitter sweet oak leaf hydrangea, plantains and gilded shells.

Hand gilding the sea shells upgrades them to first class. Now they have a grown-up, sophisticated effect. Here they are combined with the tropical and sub-tropical materials to create an opulent centerpiece.

124 - 127 PARTY IN A PEAR TREE
CONTAINER: Bronze chalice.
MATERIAL: Red pears, hypericum, protea, red Boston ivy leaves, sedum and euca-lyptus blossoms.

The pear trees are stacked up for a formal effect, but with casual materials. Again, an unlikely combination, but the color definitely pulls it all together.

128 - 131

BIRDS OF A FEATHER
CONTAINER: Antique Spanish capital.
MATERIAL: Two antique Italian cockatoos, crab apples, apples, nandina, liquid amber leaves and parrot feathers.

The lushness of the setting and the elegance of the birds needed to be overdone. The many layers of the fruits and leaves give an opulent effect without being overstated.

134 - 137

AROUND AND AROUND WE GO!
CONTAINER: Antique gilt wood urn.
MATERIAL: Privet berries, hypericum, green apples, fuji apples and roses.

Repeating the colors and patterns of the antique chinoiserie panels was the main focus. Using a traditional topiary shape and using less formal materials add to the interest of the centerpiece.

138 - 139

PROCESS OF ILLUMINATION
CONTAINER: Chartreuse porcelain plate and glass cylinders.
MATERIAL: Peas and more peas, figs, candy tuft seed heads, bittersweet, hawthorne berries and miniature protea.

The effect of a wreath of small seeds and fruits surrounding the cylinders filled with fresh peas and floating candles creates a fun pattern of all berry shapes.

140 - 141

ROOTED
CONTAINER: Glass cylinders.
MATERIAL: Ginseng roots and butterfly orchid plants.

The roots submerged under water and the orchids perched delicately on top create the illusion of plants actually growing in water.

142 - 143

BRANCHING OUT
CONTAINER: Pewter-colored fiberglass planter.
MATERIAL: Oak branches, pine tips, pine cones, ribbons and candle.

A metal topiary form, wrapped with oak branches, some still with acorns, holds a candle in a glass ball suspended from ribbons tied to the sides.

144 - 145

SNOW DRIFT
CONTAINER: Large glass flat cylinder.
MATERIAL: Dried branches, rock salt and glass icicles.

Filling the bowl with rock salt and tipping it to one side gives the effect of a snow drift. Clusters some rock salt are glued to the top to simulate snow. Icicles hanging on branches create an even more chilling winter scene.

	146 - 147 TWO'S COMPANY CONTAINER: Two antique silver urns. MATERIAL: Butternut, figs and Asian pears.	Using two small topiaries, as opposed to one large one, adds to the charm of the setting. The orange and green against the dramatic bleak background add to the drama.
	148 - 149 TIES THAT BIND CONTAINER: Antique Spanish iron candlesticks. MATERIAL: Dahlias, marigolds and jicama.	The jicama bulbs were placed on the candlesticks, then holes were carved and dahlias placed inside to create a growing effect. A garland of strung marigolds binds the two containers together. French ribbons tied and hanging add to the colorful and festive mood.
	150 - 151 RIPPLE EFFECT CONTAINER: Various sized glass bowls. MATERIAL: Flax leaves and floating candles.	The flax is woven into the sides of each bowl. It takes time, but the effect is dazzling. Fill with water and float candles. You are in for a treat!
	154 - 157 JUNGLE STORY CONTAINER: Vintage tole palm trees and bronze elephants. MATERIAL: Date palms.	This magical scene consists of date palms tucked into tole palm trees and a few bronze elephants parading on a bed of black pebbles. A safari party is just around the corner!
	158 - 161 PHEASANTLY SURPRISED CONTAINER: Silver meat tray. MATERIAL: Dusty miller, lamb's ears, eucalyptus, scabiosa pods and lots of Italian silver.	Hand gilding the sea shells upgrades them to first class. Now they have a grown-up, sophisticated effect. Here they are combined with the tropical and sub-tropical materials to create an opulent centerpiece.
	162 - 165 DINNER WITH OLD FRIENDS CONTAINER: Open table. MATERIAL: Succulents, rhododendron leaves, lotus leaves and eucalyptus pods.	A wonderful collection of old santos and crèche figures marching down the table didn't need much – so I created lotus leaf and rhododendron umbrellas held in their hands and a few succulents at their feet to anchor them.

166 - 167

MIDAS TOUCH
CONTAINER: Antique gilded jewelry display tray.
MATERIAL: Dracaena, marigolds, succulents, hypericum, miniature marigolds and iris pods.

The gilded frogs, all carrying shells on their backs, make for an amusing and interesting combination. The formal nature of the gold against the informal of the marigolds adds to the magical atmosphere.

168 - 171

IN THE ARMS OF ANGELS
CONTAINER: Two 18th-century Italian angels.
MATERIAL: Olive, bittersweet and white bougainvillea.

The wonderful angels, with bunches of branches tied to their hands and with vintage ribbon and a thin garland to connect them are the feature of this tablescape. The plant material had to be sparse so as not to overshadow them.

172 - 173

GLASS MENAGERIE
CONTAINER: Victorian fish bowl.
MATERIAL: Rock salt, glass doves, rock, crystal votives and tulips.

The bowl is filled with rock salt and two doves, while the perimeter is surrounded with rock salt for the effect of ice and snow, as well as crystal votives and two more doves. The tulips are opened and laid flat at the last minute to look like giant snow flakes. Burr!!!

174 - 177

GREAT OAKS FROM LITTLE ACORNS GROW
CONTAINER: Antique silver and gold gilt urn.
MATERIAL: Acorns, hypericum, grasses and vintage gold leaves.

The colors of magnificent old hand-painted wall panels, mostly greens, gilt and silver, are repeated in the garlands made of acorns and gilt leaves. The main urn was arranged with other materials and capped off with an old Italian drapery tieback. The antique tassel candlesticks and Venetian fruit complete the setting of the magic of old Venice.

180 - 183

SUSHI GARDEN
CONTAINER: Square Japanese plates.
MATERIAL: Tei leaves, carnations, poppy pods, tulips, fiddle fern, clover and berries.

Anything can be an inspiration. Just look around.

184 - 185

PLEASE PASS THE PEPPER
CONTAINER: Old tole cachepots.
MATERIAL: Tei leaves and red bell peppers.

Tulips being my favorite flower, I wanted them all year long. By cutting the peppers with a sharp knife, you can make tulips any time of the year. Any color of pepper will create the same effect.

186 - 187	POLKA DOT PARADE	The decision to pick up the polka dots in the china was easy. Coming up with a workable solution, however, was harder. I love the repeat of pattern from plate to plate to plate.
	CONTAINER: White China plates.	
	MATERIAL: Sunflower heads.	

188 - 191	VEGGIE PATCH	Styrofoam balls, covered in white carnations and wrapped with cabbage leaves, give the effect of large cauliflower heads, which were a fun repeat of the china plates.
	CONTAINER: Styrofoam balls.	
	MATERIAL: Carnations and cabbage leaves.	

192 - 193	ALL CHOKED UP!	Ten artichokes were separated and all the leaves were pinned to a large styrofoam ball, giving the effect of a giant artichoke in the middle of the table. Smaller artichokes surrounded by leaves and berries serve as candle holders.
	CONTAINER: Old terra cotta urn.	
	MATERIAL: Artichokes, flax, hypericum and pineapple lilies.	

194 - 197	A WALK IN THE PARK	While looking at the broccoli at the produce market, my eye saw miniature trees and shrubs. So why not add a few figurines in scale and create an instant park?
	CONTAINER: Pin frogs.	
	MATERIAL: Broccoli, aquarium gravel and bronze miniature dogs.	

198 - 201	RULER OF THE ROOST	The effect of the fruits of harvest time strewn down the table was the goal. The scale of the rooster needed large corn, so I used various-sized mums placed into carved oasis and tei leaves to create exaggerated ears of corn.
	CONTAINER: Antique French gilded shop sign.	
	MATERIAL: Chrysanthemums, tei leaves, fuji apples, persimmons and croton leaves.	

For information on Ron Morgan's lectures and his other publications,

please visit www.ronmorgandesigns.com.

RON'S 5-MINUTE LECTURE ON FLOWER CARE

1) To ensure longer flower life, cut most flowers when the color begins to show in the bud.

2) Cut flowers in the morning, when the maximum amount of moisture is in the stem.

3) Always cut flowers with a sharp knife. Roses should be cut under water. To ensure that the maximum amount of water is available to the flowers, cut the stems at a diagonal (poppies being an exception). Use warm water – at least room temperature.

4) Most hard or wood stems should either be cut with shears or mashed with a hammer before placing them into water.

5) For a longer lifespan, remove most of the foliage from most flowers.

6) Do not leave flowers standing in bright, direct sunlight as they will wilt faster.

7) To ensure crispness, submerge large flowers like hydrangeas and dahlias in water for a few minutes.

8) Use wooden (versus metal) skewers to hold elements of a table setting together. The wood expands and therefore has better holding power.

9) Use oil of cloves or oil of cinnamon on the tip of a wooden pick before inserting into fruits and vegetables. This will make them last longer.

10) Do not pack flowers too tightly into containers. Oxygen needs to get to the water's surface so that the flowers can breathe properly.

11) Never have foliage below the water line of the container. Foliage tends to rot when in direct contact with water and this will shorten the lives of the remaining flowers.

12) Most flowers do not like metal containers, as oxides are released from the containers into the water.

13) Use a fixative aerosol (a spray for charcoal or pastel paintings) on cut fruit to prevent flies and insects.

14) A shot of Sprite, or similar sugary soda, does wonders in bringing tired flowers back to life.

15) Although it is preferable to change the water daily for arrangements, it is not always practical. When it is not possible, use one teaspoon of bleach per gallon of flower water to kill the resulting bacteria. As the stems take oxygen from the water, a bacteria-ridden scum is produced. This bacteria is the single most harmful thing for all flowers. The easiest way to add water to existing floral arrangements is with a turkey baster.

221

A Heartfelt Note of Appreciation

A most sincere thanks to all the many friends and supporters who have been involved in the process of publishing IN THE COMPANY OF FLOWERS. First of all, to my "garden club ladies," who have encouraged me for years to put my thoughts and creations into book form.

Second, to Keith Lewis, whose creativity, thorough knowledge of all aspects of photography and his remarkable ability to bring flowers to life have made this book what it is.

A special thanks to Tom, for his love and support; Leslie and Rob for their encouragement and faith in me; Annabelle for her organizational and artistic talents; Joan for her persistence and wordsmithing; and David for his enthusiasm and energy.

And lastly, many, many heartfelt thanks to all of my friends who have been so generous in opening their exceptional homes to the creations in this book: Kathy, Howard, Linda, both Barbaras, Katie, Nancy, Susi, Jeanie, Kay, Ann, Suzanne, Leslie, both Janes, Sharon, Deni, Keith, Mary, Kaye, Lincoln, Chris, Tom, Camilla and Ashley.